DATE DUE

HOVERLLOYD

SWIFT

library 2000

GREAT INVENTIONS
DISCOVERIES AND INVENTIONS
FAMOUS ARTISTS AND COMPOSERS
SHIPS

Published in Great Britain by Frederick Warne (Publishers) Ltd, London, 1979
Copyright © AFHA Internacional S.A., Barcelona, Spain, 1978
English translation copyright © Frederick Warne (Publishers) Ltd, 1979

ISBN 0 7232 2341 6

Phototypeset by Tradespools Ltd, Frome, Somerset

Printed in Spain by Emograph S.A., Barcelona

library 2000

Written and illustrated by
Vincent Segrelles

Translated by John Warland

Ships

FREDERICK WARNE

CONTENTS

INTRODUCTION

From prehistoric times until the present day, mankind has had to find the answers to the riddles and difficulties posed by living and communicating. Water may once have seemed an insurmountable barrier to communication between peoples, and this is why something, a tree trunk, or a dug-out canoe, had to be found to remove this brake on human progress. Well, one day this something was discovered, we do not know by whom, and it is from that very moment that the history of ships begins.

Draught animals enabled man to cross vast distances on land. With the ship he could now communicate with other countries and other regions which had until then been shut off by the sea. We must never forget that in antiquity, the Middle Ages and modern times, culture was spread and trade grew because it was sea-borne.

Sea-power was the basis of the empires of Greece, Rome and Carthage, and the Vikings made their raids by sea. Finally it was Christopher Columbus's ships that discovered the New World.

This book uses a few nautical terms: some of these are in everyday use; others are more specialized. But all of these can be found in any general dictionary or book about sailing and this is why they have often not been explained here.

Throughout this book a mass of magnificent illustrations have been used to carry the story of ships from the raft and dug-out canoe to present-day ships. It is a highly informative and most readable history of maritime transport: one very important part of the story of human civilization.

THE FIRST BOATS

The story of the boat is as old as mankind itself. Before ever he learned to work stones, man undoubtedly discovered that a tree trunk or large branch would float in the water and support him. The real riddle that has to be solved is whether it was as much as 100,000 or possibly 50,000 years ago that men learned to collect together a number of logs to build a raft and to hollow out a tree trunk to make a canoe. Either date might well be the true one, but we simply have no firm evidence. Even today some primitive peoples use boats exactly like those of our distant ancestors. One thing is known for certain: when man first took to the water it was either in a hollowed-out log or on a simple raft.

Prehistoric man with his faithful friend the dog, on a raft made of logs.

The raft is without doubt the most ancient form of boat, built by fastening a number of logs together with creepers. A wooden pole was used which was pushed against the river bottom to drive the raft in the right direction. This was a great step forward for primitive man. The paddle must have appeared later to meet the need of crossing deeper water.

Ancient man must have noticed that a single log of wood keeps to a given direction better, for he learned to hollow it out. The dug-out canoe was thus the answer to his problem.

Below is an early raft built of bamboo, an extremely buoyant material, since the cane is naturally divided into hollow watertight compartments.

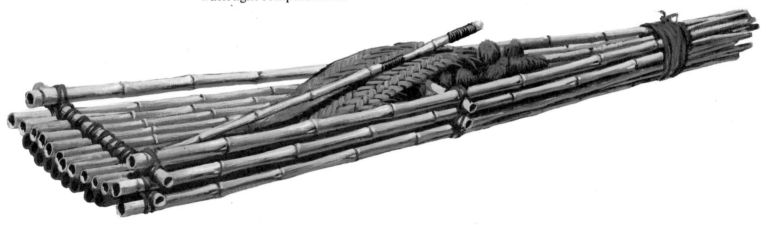

This type of raft, from the New Stone Age, is more highly developed than its forerunners. It is built over ox hides, or pig skins, sewn up, tarred and filled with air to make excellent floats.

The coracle is still used on some rivers in Wales (because of its shape it is not very seaworthy). It was the first Stone Age craft with the characteristics of the modern boat: ribs and a hull.

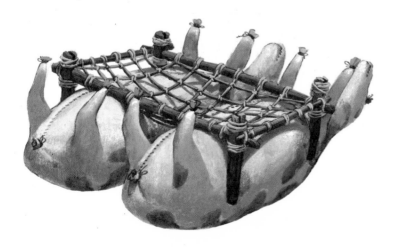

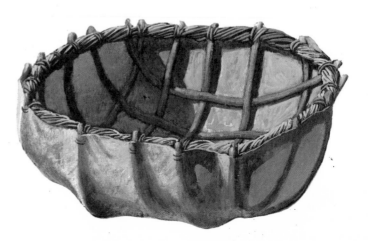

EGYPT

By 6000 or 7000 BC, the Egyptians had successfully built boats, like the one shown below, which comes from what is called the Pre-Dynastic Period. Although Egypt was not the cradle of Western civilization — which in fact sprang from Mesopotamia — she was well in the lead with boats. The Egyptians depended upon the Nile, a broad navigable river, and this forced them to find a way of travelling on it. Later came a time of political and military stagnation during which their development of the boat slowed down. This is why they were overtaken, as we shall see, by the 'Peoples of the Sea'.

Did you know . . .

. . . that the earliest Egyptian boats were rafts made of bundles of papyrus stems and not of wood?

. . . that the Egyptians slowly improved their building methods until they reached a pitch of perfection which experts even today admire?

Below we see a primitive raft made of papyrus stems. From the start the Egyptians built very serviceable boats. The way they curved and their tapered lines made them extremely useful craft.

Progress in boat building allowed the Egyptians to produce boats with wooden hulls. And so they were able to build increasingly larger and sturdier ships, like the one shown on the right (2700 BC).

Because tall trees do not grow in Egypt, boats were built with short, thick planks cut from the trunks of small acacias or sycamores. These planks were skilfully assembled and firmly held together by dovetail tenons.

A ship of the early Old Kingdom period, being large and very sturdy, was capable of voyaging on the high seas. The Egyptians nearly always used sail propulsion and when they met head winds would lower both sail and mast on to the deck. A thick cable under considerable tension ran from bow to stern. This ensured that the hull did not sag and in this way the small planks from which it was built were given added strength and solidity.

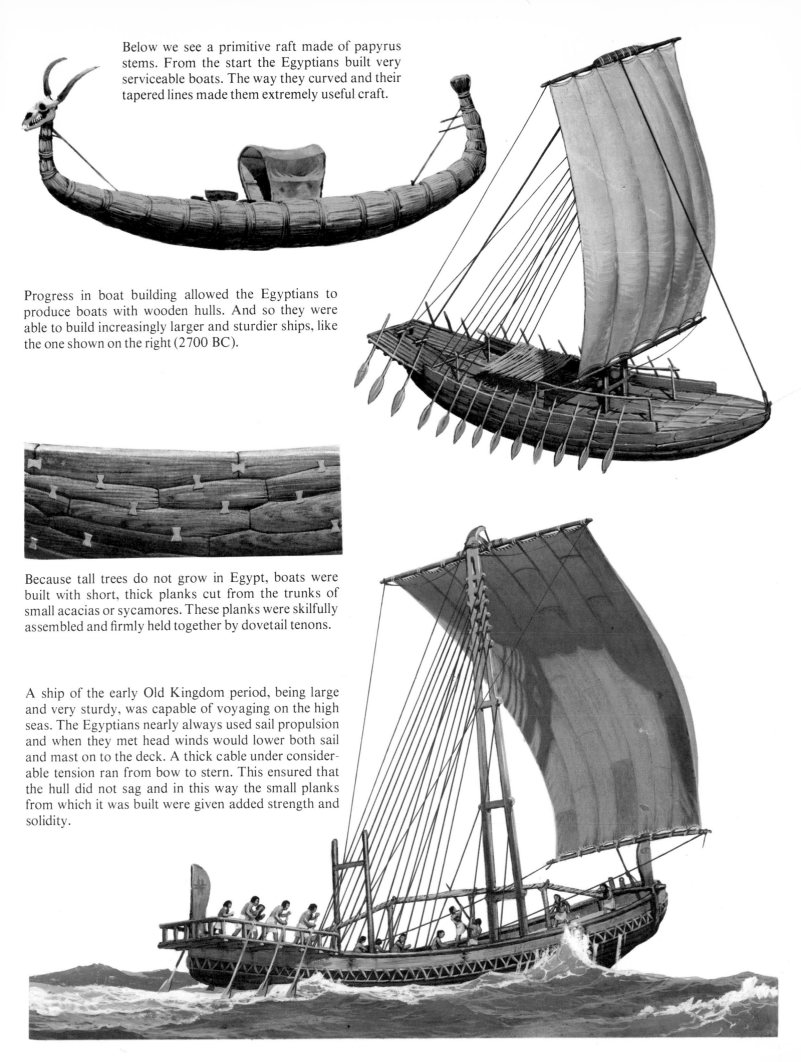

11

QUEEN HATCHEPSUT'S SHIPS

It is hardly surprising that the Egyptians, with all their love of the gigantic — remember that they built the Pyramids — should have taken to shipbuilding. All the same it must be emphasized that they were forced to do so. For example, there is the case of the huge 360-tonne obelisks, single blocks of stone hacked out of one of the quarries near Asswan — these could only be transported on the Nile. The only way of doing this was on an enormous barge like the one shown below. The only surviving picture of these barges can be seen among the bas-reliefs decorating the tomb of Queen Hatchepsut (1468 BC). It has been estimated that these barges were the largest vessels ever built in the ancient world. These technological masterpieces displaced some 1,500 tonnes and were constructed by traditional methods.

The smaller illustration shows one of the 27 vessels used to tow the barge.

THE FLEET OF RAMSES III

One day Egypt learned that the 'Peoples of the Sea', a civilization that had arisen far away to the north of them, had built better ships than their own. These peoples built their ships with keels and ribs on which they set long planks to form the hull. Their technique was based upon their use of the tall cedars of Lebanon.

At the start of the New Kingdom, the Egyptians imported cedars and adapted their shipbuilding methods to these new trends. By the time that Egypt felt the threat of the 'Peoples of the Sea', in 1200 BC, she had a fleet of these new vessels, which enabled her to meet her enemies on equal terms. In the end Ramses III was victorious and his tomb provides us with all the evidence needed to make an accurate reconstruction of these vessels.

Detail showing the rudder of one of these Egyptian vessels. It should be emphasized that this is a 'stern-rudder', an invention that was lost until the thirteenth century AD.

13

CRETE AND THE 'PEOPLES OF THE SEA'

When Crete was invaded in 1400 BC, the islanders who survived fled to the eastern Mediterranean and took with them vital knowledge of shipbuilding. Of all the Mediterranean peoples, the Phoenicians and the Egyptians were undoubtedly the Cretans' prize pupils. The Philistines, one of the tribes who made up the 'Peoples of the Sea' already mentioned, are undoubtedly among those who gave battle to the fleet of Ramses III.

Below left is a bas-relief from the tomb of Ramses III depicting one of the ships of the 'Peoples of the Sea'. Everything points to the fact that it was really the Mycenaeans who built her, since she features their all-important contributions — such as keel, ribs, cutwater and mainmast with fixed yard, the sail being hoisted from the deck.

Did you know . . .

. . . that the Philistines of the story of David and Goliath in the Bible, were a people who had migrated from Crete to settle on the southern coast of Palestine in the twelfth century BC?

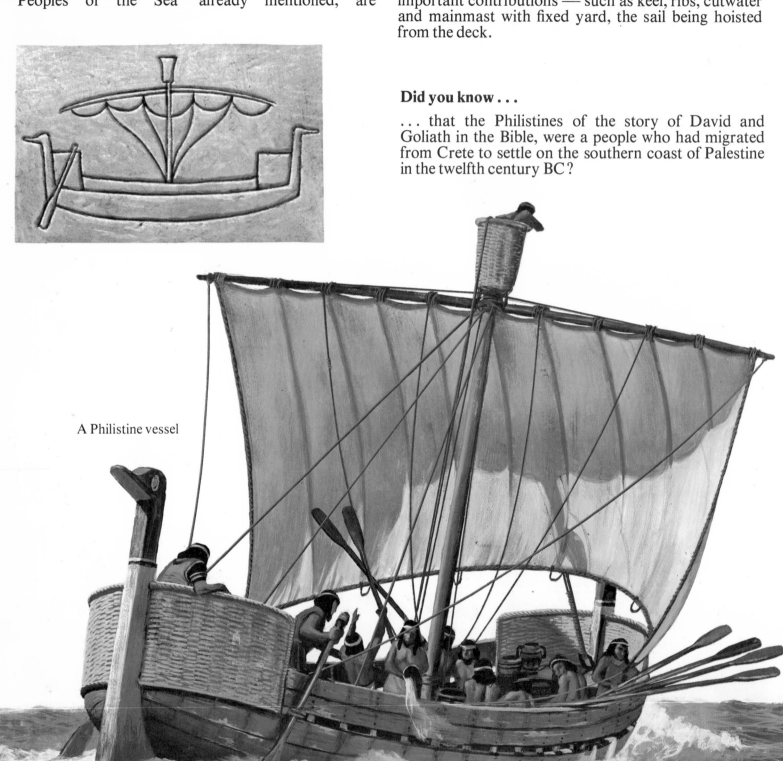

A Philistine vessel

THE PHOENICIANS

Their isolated position on the Mediterranean coast forced the Phoenicians to live by fishing, trade and piracy. Over the years they built up a sizeable fleet and we can credit the Phoenicians with being great sailors.

Phoenician merchant ships looked very much like Egyptian vessels, but being built of cedar of Lebanon they were much tougher and better fitted for sailing the high seas.

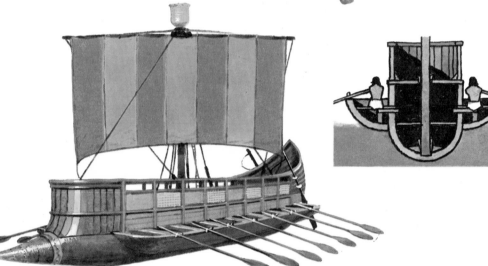

This type of galley was built by the Phoenicians to guard their trade routes and was very probably the earliest example of a purpose-built warship. It was made by hollowing a massive cedar trunk and adding two half-hulls to give it stability, thus producing a very tough and speedy vessel — essential qualities if her ram was to be driven home into the enemy ship.

Their Phoenician blood made the Carthaginians great seamen. They built big strong ships able to withstand the Mediterranean storms.

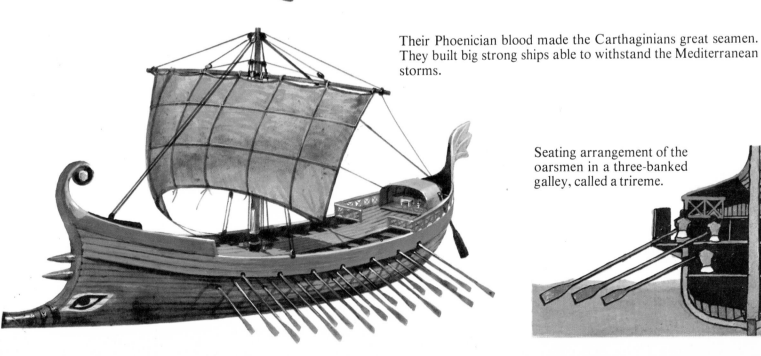

Seating arrangement of the oarsmen in a three-banked galley, called a trireme.

THE GREEKS AND THE ROMANS

The Greeks were without doubt the most daring master-mariners of the ancient world. And men of such outstanding qualities had ships to match: seamen such as Euthymenes and Pytheas would never have explored the west coast of Africa and north along the Atlantic seaboard if they hadn't also had excellent strongly-built ships.

The Greek merchant ships that sailed the high seas were dual purpose. In other words they were used both for trade and fighting, the latter because they had to contend with pirates. Throughout Classical times the only sail was the square sail. This was because merchant ships carried very small crews and rowing was obviously tiring. On the other hand, because of the battle tactics of the period, a powerful body of oarsmen was what counted on board a warship.

Did you know . . .

. . . that the Greeks had the lightest and most stylish warships in the ancient world; so light in fact that their crews were able to lift them up and beach them on the shore?

. . . that the Romans were quite unoriginal in their shipbuilding, being content to copy the Greeks and Carthaginians to start with; although later on their enterprise led them to design ships of their own?

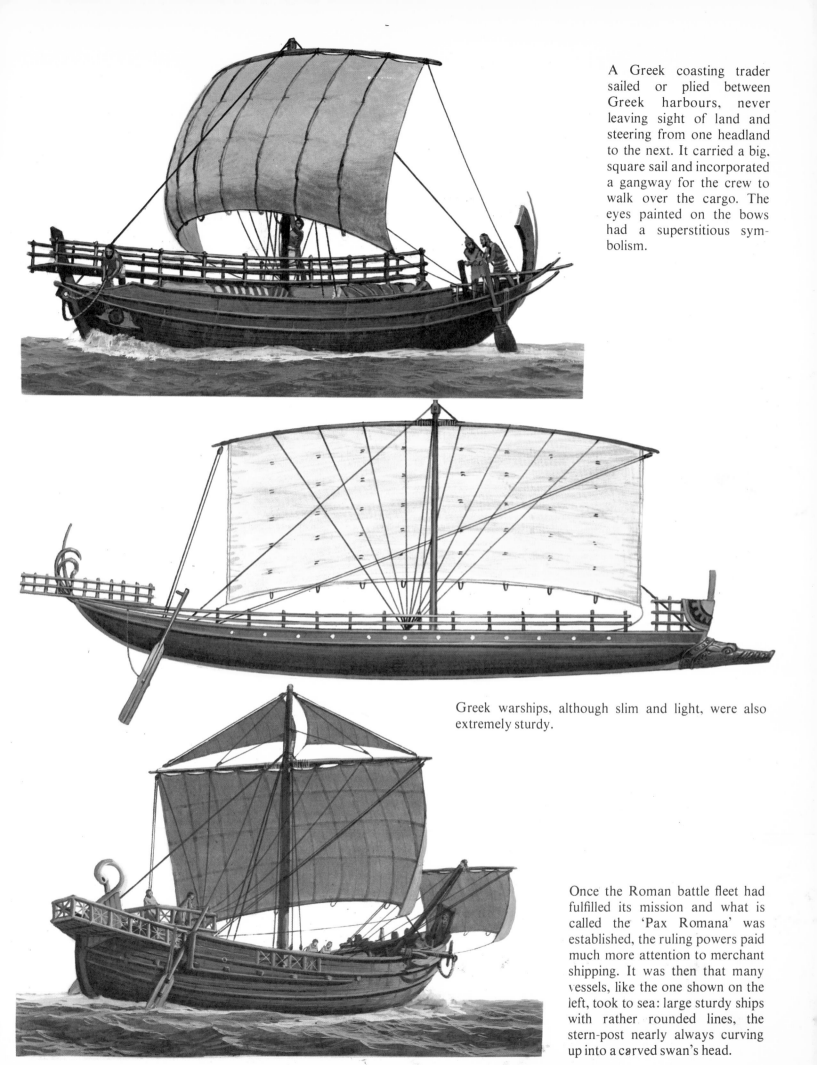

A Greek coasting trader sailed or plied between Greek harbours, never leaving sight of land and steering from one headland to the next. It carried a big, square sail and incorporated a gangway for the crew to walk over the cargo. The eyes painted on the bows had a superstitious symbolism.

Greek warships, although slim and light, were also extremely sturdy.

Once the Roman battle fleet had fulfilled its mission and what is called the 'Pax Romana' was established, the ruling powers paid much more attention to merchant shipping. It was then that many vessels, like the one shown on the left, took to sea: large sturdy ships with rather rounded lines, the stern-post nearly always curving up into a carved swan's head.

17

NORSE SHIPS

The Mediterranean was not the only sea on which man went sailing. Every early centre of civilization used the boat as a means of transport. A flourishing civilization sprang up in northern Europe and although it was somewhat behind the Mediterranean peoples, it, too, developed a powerful maritime force, since it was from the sea that it drew so much of its livelihood.

The earliest Scandinavian boats date from about 3000 BC. These were the traditional dug-out canoes hollowed from a tree trunk. By 1500 BC the peoples of the North were using canoes of animal hides over a light wooden framework. From these canoes were developed over the centuries the famous 'drakkars', the 'dragon-ships' of the Vikings of the eighth and ninth centuries AD. These formidable vessels were built with overlapping planks (clinker-built). Swift and seaworthy, their appearance on the horizon sowed terror along the whole Atlantic seaboard. They were equipped with shrouds — stout supporting ropes running from the sides of the ship to the masthead — from which we know that the Vikings sailed into head and cross-winds. Further development of the Norse ship into the 'cog', affected the whole future progress of ship design.

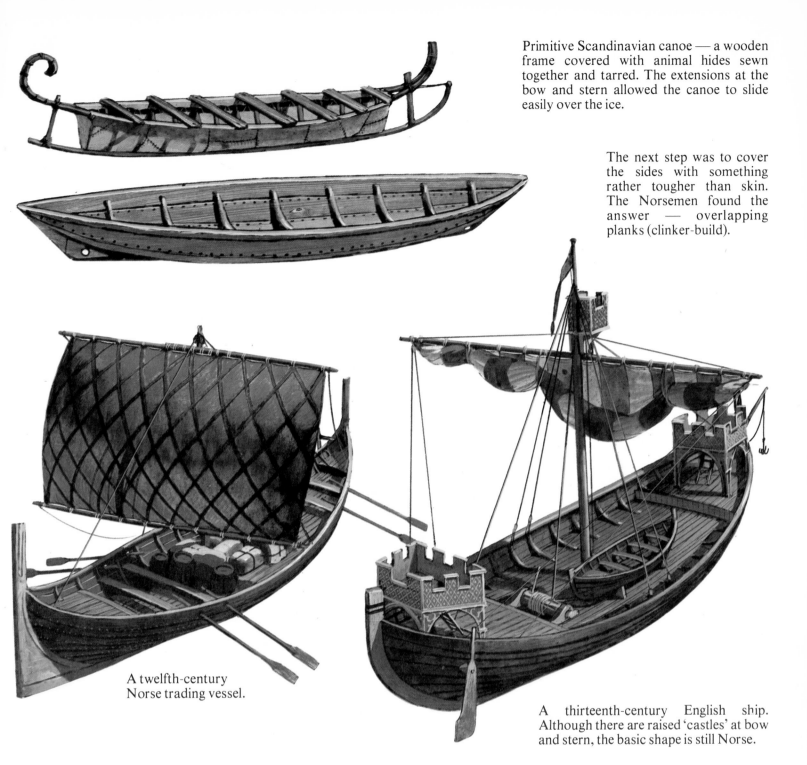

Primitive Scandinavian canoe — a wooden frame covered with animal hides sewn together and tarred. The extensions at the bow and stern allowed the canoe to slide easily over the ice.

The next step was to cover the sides with something rather tougher than skin. The Norsemen found the answer — overlapping planks (clinker-build).

A twelfth-century Norse trading vessel.

A thirteenth-century English ship. Although there are raised 'castles' at bow and stern, the basic shape is still Norse.

A detail of a clinker-built hull. This provided a stronger and more watertight hull than contemporary Mediterranean shipbuilding methods, but it was impractical for large vessels. So the Norsemen later had to adopt the southern 'carvel-built' technique in which the edges of the strakes (planks) are flush with one another.

The Gotland drawing. It shows us the arrival on the scene of the single, centre-line stern rudder instead of the traditional steering oars on either side of the stern.

MEDIEVAL CHINESE JUNKS

China, as well as the Western world, was an important cradle of civilization, and although when Marco Polo reached the Celestial Empire in the thirteenth century he found their ships were strange to look at, they were highly practical and efficient. What he saw, of course, were junks. They were, and still are — for they have changed hardly at all over the centuries — large, flexible vessels, characterized by their lug-sails, their size and their easy handling. In the thirteenth century they were far in advance of any European vessels. However their development came to a halt with the decay of the Chinese Empire.

Did you know . . .

. . . that in the time of Marco Polo the Chinese had long perfected an efficient centre-line rudder, which shows that, as in so many other things, they were technically ahead of the Europeans?

20

THE LATEEN SAIL

In the early Middle Ages the type of sail shown in the illustration on the left was first seen on the Mediterranean Sea. The lateen is a 'fore and aft' sail, since it is set along a line running from the forepart of the ship aft. Nobody quite knows where it came from. Some say from the Arabs, others that it derives from the Chinese lug-sail, and others that it came from India. What is certain is that it is a very efficient sail which can work 50 or 60 degrees into the wind. It therefore rapidly replaced the classical square sail which only worked when the wind was more or less dead astern. Later on northern influence restored the square sail to the Mediterranean once more, where it was combined with the lateen, especially on ships which crossed the Atlantic.

In the thirteenth century command of the Mediterranean was shared between the city states of Genoa, Pisa, Venice, Marseilles and Barcelona. All merchant ships (right), except for very slight differences, looked exactly the same. They were clumsy, tubby craft propelled by a pair of lateen sails and steered by two stern oars. For 100 years ship design stood still: the hull forms were still exactly the same as those of the Roman ships of the Classical age.

From the thirteenth century until the Battle of Lepanto (1571), the galley remained the predominant type of warship, and battle tactics were still those of the Romans — to ram and board the enemy vessel — with the sole exception that the ram itself was no longer set at the waterline, but clear of it. Boarding was made easier and, as the enemy ship was not sunk, she could be incorporated into her captor's fleet. Like merchant ships, galleys carried lateen sails.

THE STERN RUDDER

While the rudder came into general use along the Atlantic, in the Mediterranean ships were still steered by a pair of oars at the stern until the fourteenth-century when they were replaced by the northern invention. No evidence from this period has survived to tell us how ships were built, for in those days ship-builders made no plans or drawings. Shipwrights simply put their vessels together by well-tried rule-of-thumb methods, passed down from one generation to the next by word-of-mouth — the method still used in small boatyards today. This is why in 1920 so much importance was placed upon the discovery of a genuine mid-fourteenth-century model of a ship made originally for a votive offering to the shrine of Saint Simon of Mataró near Barcelona (illustrated below).

Most seamen were not expert wood-carvers, and so their models were often clumsy and out of scale. However, their efforts show us what ships of that period were really like.

Did you know...

... that making votive models was a very old custom among seamen who really enjoyed making models of the ships in which they had survived so many dangers?

... that when they had come safely through a bad storm, sailors would offer a votive model to the church or shrine of the saint to whom they had called for aid in their peril?

A reconstruction of the votive model shown on page 22.

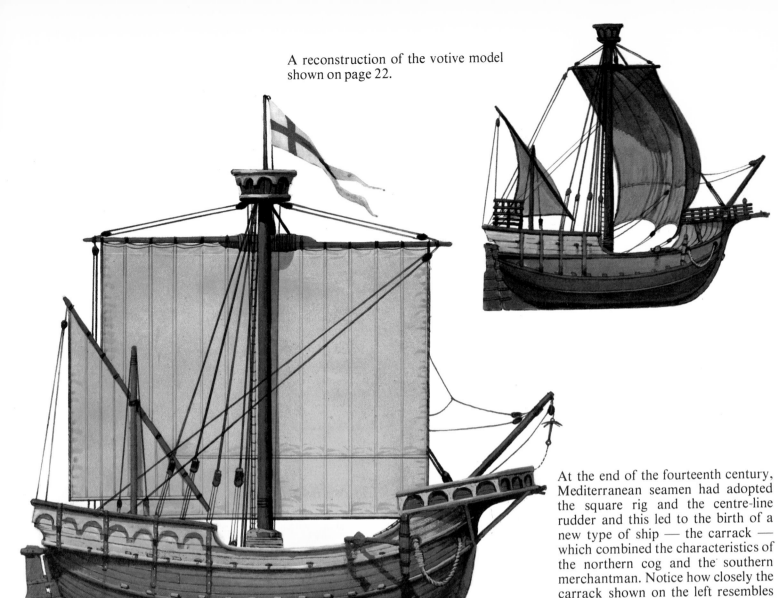

At the end of the fourteenth century, Mediterranean seamen had adopted the square rig and the centre-line rudder and this led to the birth of a new type of ship — the carrack — which combined the characteristics of the northern cog and the southern merchantman. Notice how closely the carrack shown on the left resembles the votive model from Mataró. The model is in fact an early prototype of the carrack.

The introduction of the centre-line rudder and other typical characteristics of the carrack may have come about in the following way. One day, in the middle of the fourteenth century, a large merchantman tied up in the port of Barcelona. It was a stranger, with unfamiliar lines and rig — a 'cog' from Bayonne in southwestern France, with centre-line rudder, square sail and strong shrouds. The Catalan shipwrights took a very careful look at it, copied it and adapted its lines in their own vessels. Later on other countries copied the Catalans and from these vessels the carrack developed.

THE RISE AND FALL OF THE CARRACK

Although the carrack was a broad-beamed, lumbering vessel, it was sturdy, capacious and handy. It therefore proved an excellent merchant ship. However, the slowness of the carrack made it liable to fall prey to the swarms of pirate galleys which haunted the seaways, and hence these vessels were armed with cannon. The ship's guns of the period were not very accurate and so the fore- and after-castles were heightened to make boarding more difficult and to provide rallying-points.

By the beginning of the sixteenth century, carracks of considerable size were being built—some of as much as 1,000 tonnes displacement. This was the age of the birth of the nation states and of the opening of the trade routes to the East. Because of its short range, the galley proved useless as a warship, and the carrack was developed to take its place. In doing this the height of the castles was raised and more and more guns were mounted in them. This in its turn raised the centre of gravity and made the vessels liable to capsize. Shipwrights therefore had to look for a new approach.

The combination of square and lateen sail made a vast improvement in the performance of sailing ships. A sail plan based on three masts and a bowsprit became the standard pattern. On the other hand, hull design lagged. The illustration on the right, of the cross-section of a carrack's stern, shows the large number of gun decks and her pronounced 'tumble home'. By sloping the sides inwards in this way, boarding, the standard battle tactic of the period, was made more difficult.

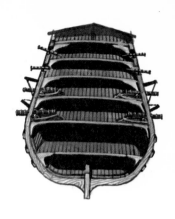

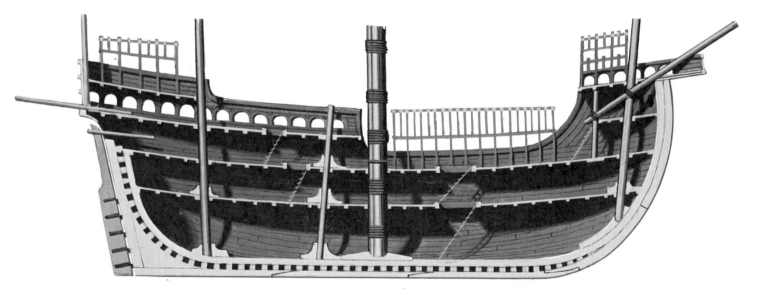

Cross-section of a carrack of around 1500.

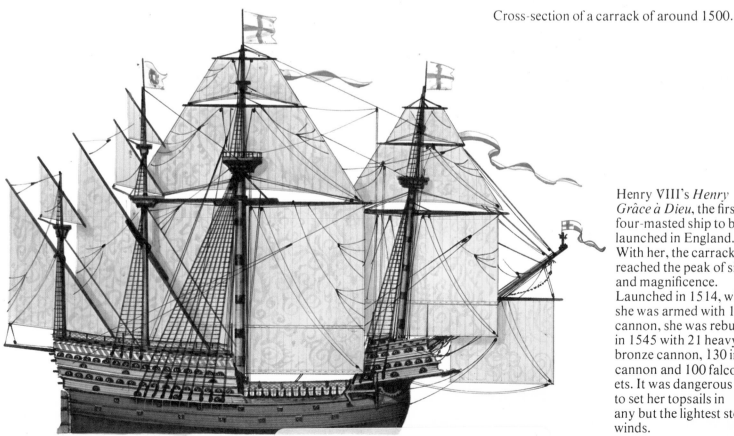

Henry VIII's *Henry Grâce à Dieu*, the first four-masted ship to be launched in England. With her, the carrack reached the peak of size and magnificence. Launched in 1514, when she was armed with 184 cannon, she was rebuilt in 1545 with 21 heavy bronze cannon, 130 iron cannon and 100 falconets. It was dangerous to set her topsails in any but the lightest stern winds.

CHRISTOPHER COLUMBUS'S SQUADRON

Because so little written evidence has come down to us from the period, nobody can be really certain about Christopher Columbus's ships. Some say that his *Santa Maria* was a carrack, others that she was a caravel, and others again that she was a different type of ship altogether. All, however, agree that the *Pinta* and the *Niña* were caravels. A probable explanation is that the *Santa Maria* was a new type of vessel which Columbus himself simply called a 'nef' and whose enormous potential he appreciated. The 'nef' may perhaps have combined the hull of the caravel with the rigging of the carrack, so enjoying the advantages of both types, while avoiding their disadvantages. Proof of these advantages lies in the fact that Columbus's 'nef' reached a speed of between 3.75 and 5 knots. When one remembers that Nelson's ships-of-the-line were hard pushed to reach 6 knots, it is easily realized that the *Santa Maria* managed a respectable speed.

Did you know . . .

. . . that Columbus missed making a landfall on the American mainland simply because, instead of following his predetermined course, he adopted Martín Pinzón's suggestion that they should follow the flight-path of a flock of birds?

The fifteenth-century caravel carried lateen sails. The lines of her hull were much finer than those of the carrack and this made her a better sea boat. She also drew more water, which helped. Her bows were still too blunt to slice through the water like those of the clippers were to do in years to come. The caravel was to develop along her own lines to produce a very different type of vessel from the *Santa Maria*, as can be seen from the illustrations on the left.

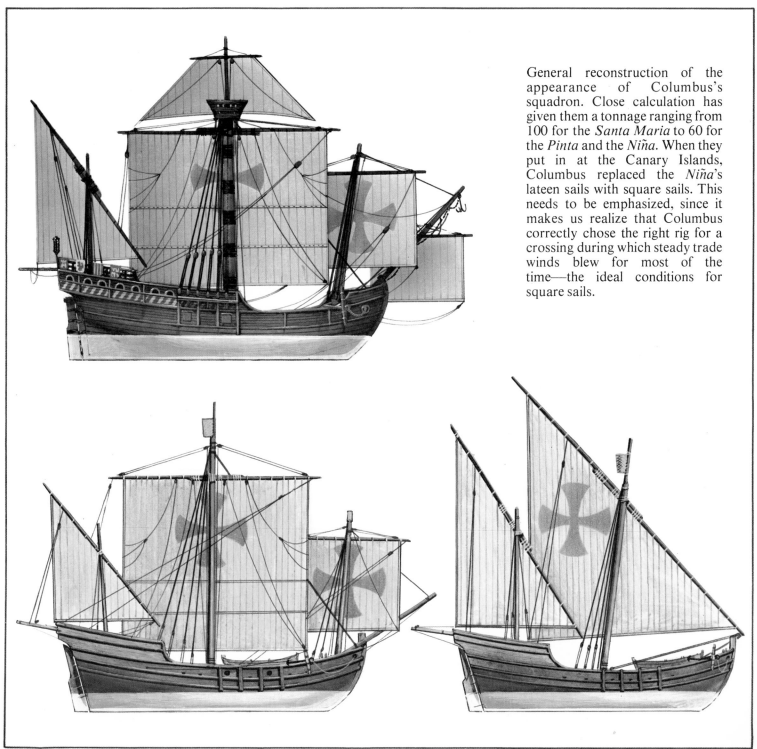

General reconstruction of the appearance of Columbus's squadron. Close calculation has given them a tonnage ranging from 100 for the *Santa Maria* to 60 for the *Pinta* and the *Niña*. When they put in at the Canary Islands, Columbus replaced the *Niña*'s lateen sails with square sails. This needs to be emphasized, since it makes us realize that Columbus correctly chose the right rig for a crossing during which steady trade winds blew for most of the time—the ideal conditions for square sails.

THE GALLEON

Nobody quite knows how the galleon originated. Perhaps she goes back to Columbus's 'nef' and ships similar to her. The Spaniard Alvaro de Bazán was marginally involved in the design of the galleon as a warship, that is in its armament and defences. All that is definitely known is that the galleon first appeared in Spain and that she ruled the seas from the sixteenth to the beginning of the seventeenth century. She started out as a small merchant vessel armed to withstand attack by pirates and then grew into the large warship which was the backbone of all the fleets of Europe.

Since boarding was still the main battle tactic, her castles were raised and her 'tumble home' was as pronounced as that of the carrack. The ram was obsolete. The English relied more upon gunfire than boarding and for this reason built their galleons with lower castles and a greater draught. As a result of this they offered a smaller target and also a more stable platform for heavier guns with a longer range, which they mounted on their galleons. Because they did not carry soldiers their decks were free for the sailors to work the ship.

A typical feature of the galleon was the timbers projecting beyond the bows at deck level. In the very beginning these timbers derived from the ram in the bows of the galleass, but from the ram they developed over the years into a flat platform supported by pieces raking upwards and outwards from the stem on which the figurehead stood. The heads was the place where the crew's latrines were situated. This is a feature which afterwards became common to all sailing ships, including the clippers.

By the sixteenth century detailed plans ensured the high standards of shipbuilding.

The traditional warship, the galley, gradually became obsolete, although most Mediterranean sea powers continued to use them. The Battle of Lepanto in 1571 was the last full-scale action at sea fought by galleys. The Christians owed their victory over the Turks to the presence in their fleet of six galleasses: big, robust, three-masted galleys, armed with heavy cannon and carrying a strong contingent of soldiers.

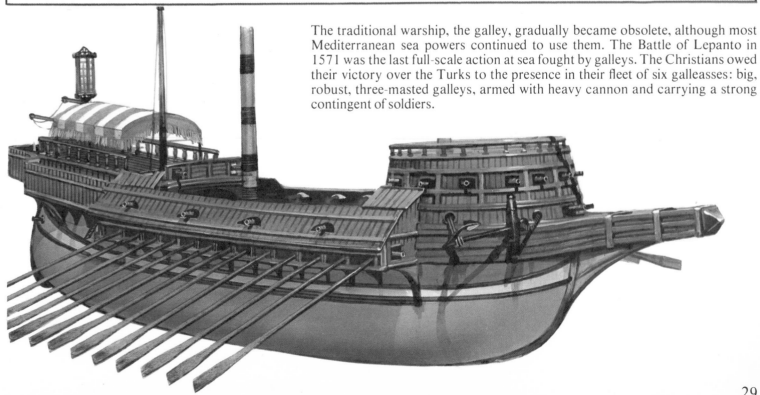

DUTCH SEA POWER

Since the Dutch only began to build a colonial empire at the end of the sixteenth century, they lagged far behind the Spaniards and the Portuguese, who had divided the New World and the Indies between them. All Europe was infected by the fever of colonization, in which the Dutch, since they had a long tradition of seamanship, soon took a leading part.

Shown below is the commonest Dutch merchant ship of the period, the hooker. Dutch warships were slightly smaller and better armed vessels, called pinnaces. These they used to convoy their merchantmen and, like the other countries which had done badly in the colonial share-out, Holland also employed pinnaces as freebooters, particularly against Spain and Portugal.

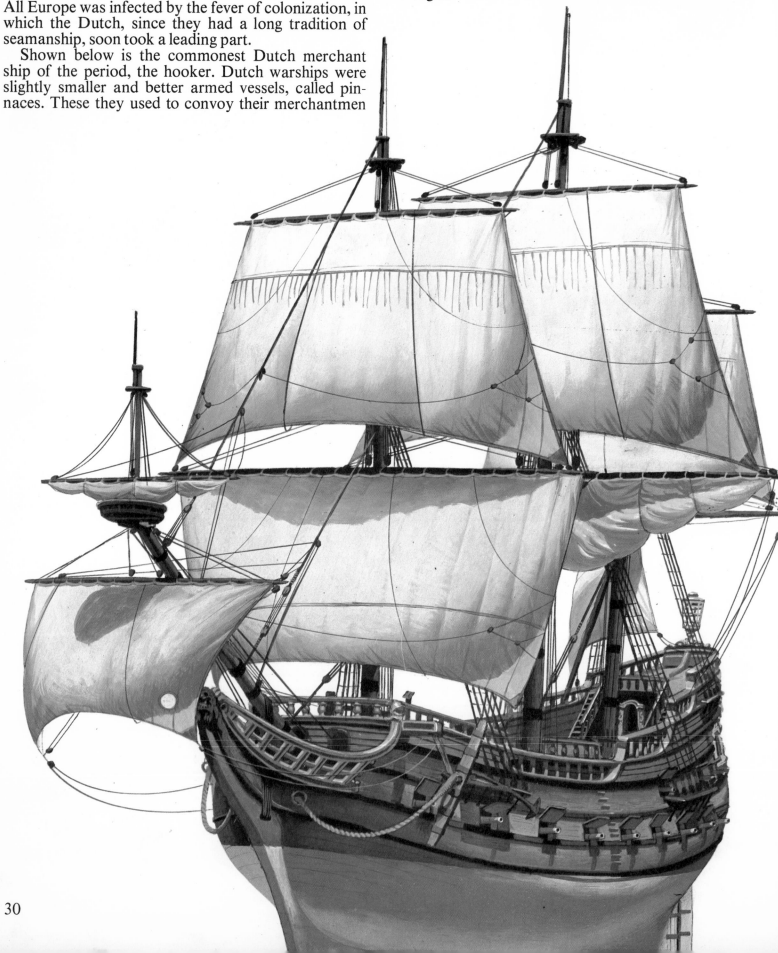

Because its fleet was so huge, Holland suffered from a shortage of seamen. The Dutch therefore made the rigging of their ships simpler and only set two sails on each mast. This enabled them to reduce the crew of a 100-tonne vessel to ten men, compared with English crews of 30.

Up to that time the helmsman had been below deck, but now he was given a direct view of the sails (above).

By the beginning of the eighteenth century the Dutch were using small, fast, single-masted vessels. By the middle of the century these were starting to carry gaff sails, a rig which was later to become very important. The Dutch called the vessels yachts, and when King Charles II of England purchased one for his own amusement, he was starting a trend which would grow into the worldwide sport of yachting.

This is the oldest surviving plan of a vessel from this period. It is dated 1670 and the frame of this pinnace is clearly drawn so that it is easy to make out her lines.

THE EIGHTEENTH-CENTURY SHIP-OF-THE-LINE

When describing the galleon it was noted that the English had evolved a new system of battle tactics which enabled them to beat their enemies at sea. Widespread use of more accurate cannon with a longer range led to boarding being replaced by the artillery duel (the broadside), and when all the battle fleets adopted this tactic it meant the appearance of a new sort of warship—the line-of-battle ship, or ship-of-the-line. Based on the English style of galleon, it produced something new and distinctive. This was the start of a breed of warships which held the seas until the middle of the nineteenth century. The most important change was the overall increase in size which enabled ships to carry large numbers of heavy cannon. Typical features of these vessels were the flusher lines of the deck as the fore- and aft-castles disappeared; the gradual rounding of the beak until it lost all resemblance to the ram from which it had developed; and the heavy gilding.

The *Prince Royal*

The new trends in shipbuilding came to a head in 1610 when the *Prince Royal* was launched. This famous vessel was the work of the skilled shipwright Phineas Pett and originally carried 56 guns, although later her armament was increased to 90. In 1637, on the orders of Charles I, Pett built the biggest warship of her age. Her 70m length overall and armament of 100 guns was not to be overtaken for 100 years. She was the *Sovereign of the Seas*, nicknamed 'The Golden Devil' because of the huge amount of gilding on her upper works. In fact this was so heavy that most of it had to be removed. After coming victorious through seven fleet actions, she was accidentally burnt in 1696, rebuilt in 1701 and finally broken up in 1763.

The *Sovereign of the Seas*

A French ship-of-the-line

The other European powers followed the English in building line-of-battle ships and the French are generally accepted as having had the edge over their rivals in their construction. This could not overcome the English superiority as fighting sailors.

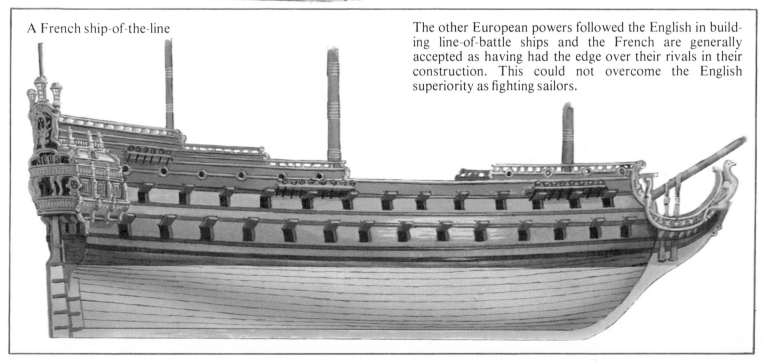

SMALL WARSHIPS

Line-of-battle ships, which bore the brunt and took the glory of fleet actions, were divided into four classes, or 'rates', based upon their armament, from the 60-gun fourth-rates to the first-rates of 90 guns and more. There were also fifth- and sixth-rates, and also a number of unrated classes which like them took no part in general actions. They all had their special duties, typical among them being the bomb-ship, shown below. This was a small, stoutly built vessel which, in place of a fore-mast, carried a couple of mortars, throwing 90kg shells. It was used for close-range bombardment of shore defences.

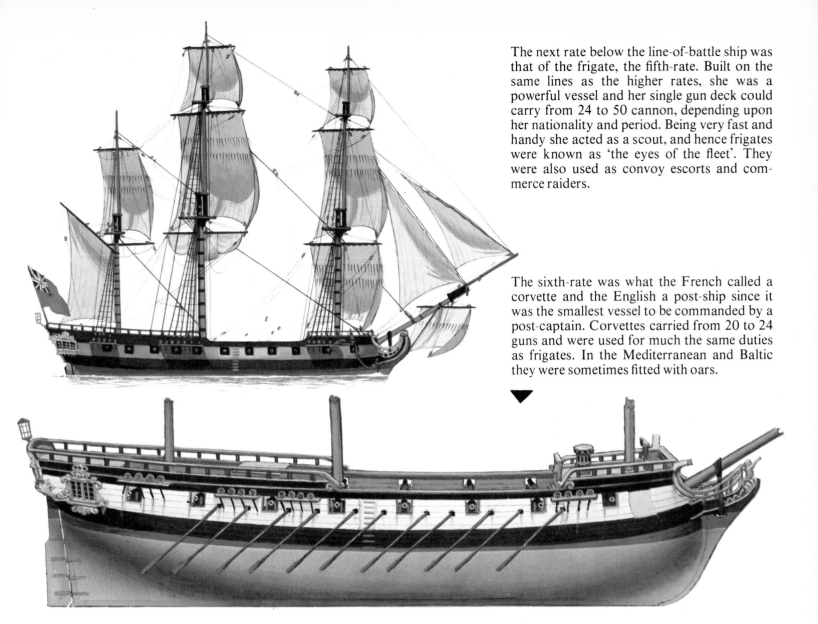

The next rate below the line-of-battle ship was that of the frigate, the fifth-rate. Built on the same lines as the higher rates, she was a powerful vessel and her single gun deck could carry from 24 to 50 cannon, depending upon her nationality and period. Being very fast and handy she acted as a scout, and hence frigates were known as 'the eyes of the fleet'. They were also used as convoy escorts and commerce raiders.

The sixth-rate was what the French called a corvette and the English a post-ship since it was the smallest vessel to be commanded by a post-captain. Corvettes carried from 20 to 24 guns and were used for much the same duties as frigates. In the Mediterranean and Baltic they were sometimes fitted with oars.

The brig was a small, unrated vessel armed with from 10 to 16 guns. It was a fast and handy two-masted craft of square- or mixed-rig, and was used as a dispatch boat.

The cutter was a small, single-masted, unrated English warship, carrying a gaff mainsail, jibs and sometimes a square topsail. Used as patrol boats, particularly in the war of the Customs against smugglers, cutters reached a fair size and in the eighteenth century some were even big enough to carry 12 guns or 4 carronades.

FISHING BOATS AND WHALERS

Throughout the ages man has always fished and used vessels to hunt his food on the seas. In the ancient world fishing boats were always very small and carried the widest range of rigs according to time and place. By the eighteenth century a growing number of large fishing boats were sailing the world's waters, specially designed for such specific tasks as herring- or cod-fishing. Once fishing such distant latitudes as the North Atlantic Ocean's Newfoundland Banks started, the need arose for large, fast, wide-ranging vessels in which the catch could be salted so that it could be preserved in a fresh condition on the long voyage home. By the seventeenth century the Dutch, whose prosperity was founded on their fishing fleet, had started to hunt the whale in the Arctic seas. Whaling was an exciting but extremely dangerous undertaking, and many men lost their lives in pursuit of these enormous beasts.

Seventeenth-century whalers were real floating factories. The illustration on the right shows blubber being stripped from a dead whale. It was then rendered down and barrelled. Below are shown the tool used to flense (cut up) the whale, and various types of harpoon head.

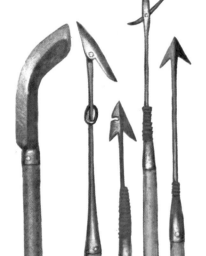

Below is shown a whale-boat, from which the harpooners plied their difficult and dangerous trade of chasing and eventually killing their valuable catch.

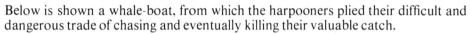

Massive shoals of cod attracted the fishing fleets of many nations to the Newfoundland Grand Banks. Fishery protection vessels policed these waters to prevent quarrels.

Eighteenth-century chart of the main cod-fishing grounds.

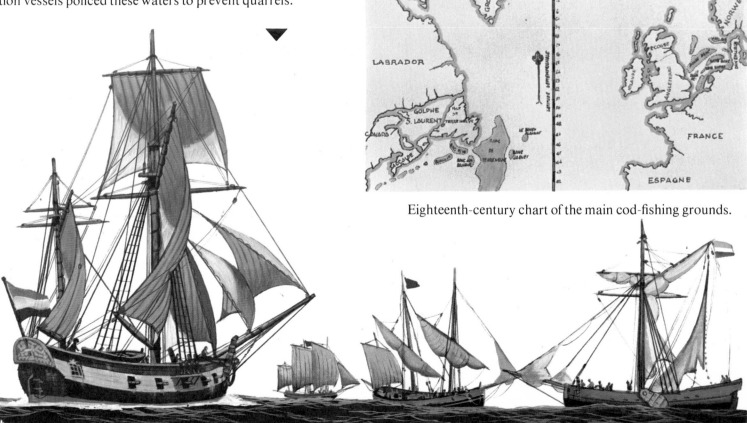

EIGHTEENTH-CENTURY MERCHANT SHIPS

The trading vessels which ranged the oceans of the world were built on the same roomy lines as the warships of the period. The majority had roughly the same size and appearance as frigates, although they were more lightly armed. For the coasting trade within European waters there was a whole range of smaller craft which developed local types and rigs.

The longest sea routes were those to the East, and the Dutch, English and French East India Companies built Indiamen (merchant ships the size of ships-of-the-line) to make the lengthy voyage. There were very few ports of call on the route and the rich cargoes carried attracted pirates and privateers. These large Indiamen were therefore well armed and their crews were highly disciplined.

The frigate-like hull of an eighteenth-century ocean-going merchant ship.

The Swedish snow, a medium-sized merchant ship trading originally in northern waters. It is similar to the brig, the main difference being that the boom mainsail does not traverse on the mainmast but on a trysail mast immediately behind it.

A French lugger, so called because it carried lug-sails. These swift sailing vessels were the favourites of Channel privateersmen and smugglers. Luggers were also used by French Customs officers.

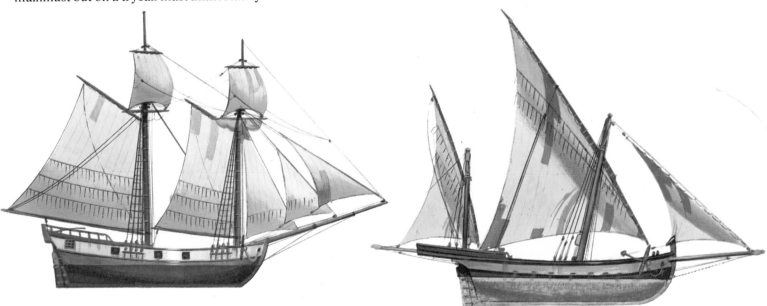

In the seventeenth century the Dutch invented the galley (a sailing, not an oared vessel), but this forerunner of all fore-and-aft rigged ships had to wait a century before it developed its potential as the schooner. The vessel pictured above is a topsail schooner with gaff mainsails and square topsails.

The felucca, a Mediterranean vessel of about 100 tonnes. As a coaster, she did not need to carry any armament, relying on her speed to get her out of trouble. The felucca derived from the swift-sailing xebecs of the sixteenth century, small, three-masted vessels used by Arab pirates.

HMS *VICTORY*

HMS *Victory*, Nelson's flagship at the Battle of Trafalgar in 1805, today lies in dry dock at Portsmouth. Scrupulously restored, her black and yellow sides, gun decks, companionways and cabins are redolent of her past glories. Nelson died on board the *Victory* during the battle.

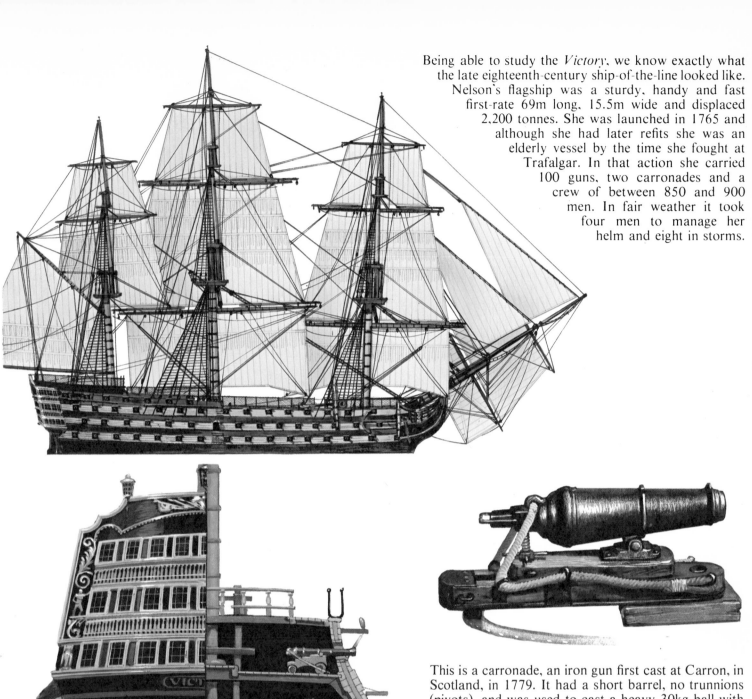

Being able to study the *Victory*, we know exactly what the late eighteenth-century ship-of-the-line looked like. Nelson's flagship was a sturdy, handy and fast first-rate 69m long, 15.5m wide and displaced 2,200 tonnes. She was launched in 1765 and although she had later refits she was an elderly vessel by the time she fought at Trafalgar. In that action she carried 100 guns, two carronades and a crew of between 850 and 900 men. In fair weather it took four men to manage her helm and eight in storms.

This is a carronade, an iron gun first cast at Carron, in Scotland, in 1779. It had a short barrel, no trunnions (pivots), and was used to cast a heavy 30kg ball with devastating effect at close range.

The hulls of wooden ships were particularly subject to attack by worms. In the eighteenth century ships' bottoms were protected with sheathing and *Victory*'s hull was sheathed with copper.

Ship's cannon were mounted on stout wooden carriages and ranged from 40 to 300mm calibre depending on which gun deck they stood. Their tremendous recoil on discharge was taken up by thick ropes.

CLIPPERS

The short but brilliant career of the clipper sums up all the speed, style and beauty of ocean sailing. These vessels developed from the fast schooners built in the USA's Baltimore shipyards at the beginning of the nineteenth century, although they did not reach their full form until some 50 years later. Although some clippers worked on for many years, by the end of the nineteenth century they had become completely outdated. Many books have been filled with the stories of their adventurous voyages and they have now passed into the realm of legend.

This speedy and highly versatile little topsail schooner was launched in Baltimore, Chesapeake Bay, to become one of the famous Baltimore clippers, forerunners of the true clipper ships.

Launched in New York in 1845, the *Rainbow* is considered to have been the first true clipper. She had three masts with a large suit of sails and a raking prow and concave bow section. Later on the hull was given longer, more slender lines.

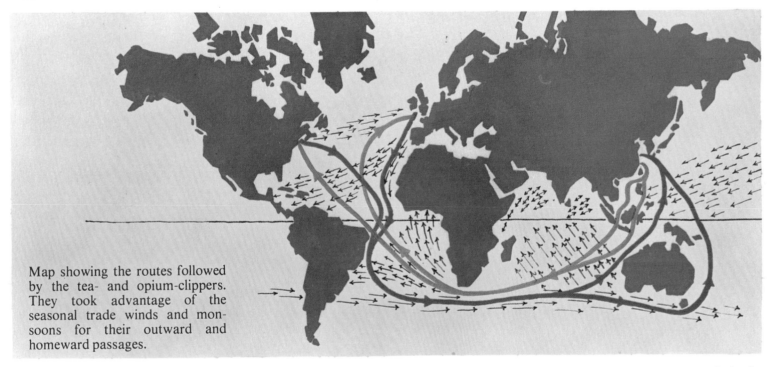

Map showing the routes followed by the tea- and opium-clippers. They took advantage of the seasonal trade winds and monsoons for their outward and homeward passages.

Hull of the clipper *Cutty Sark*, famous for the part she played in the tea races from China and the wool races from Australia. She is now preserved in dry dock at Greenwich. Launched in 1869, she was designed to beat the champion of the period, the *Thermopylae*, but never succeeded in doing so. She measures 65m in length and 10.7m in breadth and displaced 921 tonnes.

THE LAST OF THE SAILING SHIPS

Once the exciting days of the clippers were over, merchant seamen had to face the truth that steamers were improving all the time, and the owners of sailing ships realized that they would have to cut their costs if they were to remain competitive. This ushered in the age of the fore-and-aft schooner, since this rig needed a much smaller crew to work the ship. The fore-and-aft schooner gradually drove out the square-rigger. At that time it was thought that 500 tonnes was the limit for the schooner; however, the Americans built big five- six-

and seven-masted schooners, such as the steel-hulled *Thomas W Lawson*, shown above. She displaced 5,218 tonnes and used steam winches for sail handling. Built in 1902, she saw service for only five years before capsizing off the Scilly Isles.

Did you know ...

... that the American schooner *Thomas W Lawson*, with seven 59m-high masts, had a crew of only 16?

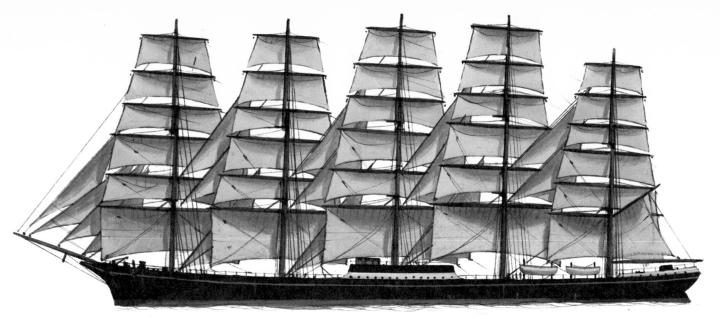

The German vessel *Preussen* was one of the biggest barks of all time. She was launched in 1902, with the steel hull, mast and wire ropes of the period, measured 124m overall and displaced 11,150 tonnes fully loaded. The surface area of her sails when fully set was 5,575 square metres, the greatest sail-surface ever known.

One of the largest of the square-riggers, the *Archibald Russel*, was launched in 1905. There are a few square-riggers still in service as naval training ships. A few of them are survivors of the days of sail, but most have been built more recently.

In the middle of the nineteenth century brigs were used as small ocean-going vessels. Eventually they were put to work as colliers in the English Channel.

The three-masted topsail schooner. These fast vessels had the advantage of both rigs, but needed larger crews than the fore-and-aft type schooner.

The fast fishing schooner *Elsie*, an ancestor of the modern ocean-racing yacht, was launched in 1910 and displaced 98 tonnes. She was built for speed to race the rest of the fleet to and from the fishing grounds.

STEAM

In August 1807, a steamship 42m long headed up the USA's Hudson River, making a great deal of noise and puffing out clouds of smoke. She managed to cover 241km in 32 hours. This was the *Clermont*, the first steamship to enter the history of sailing.

Did you know...

... that within five years of the *Clermont*'s first voyage, 50 steamers were working on the inland waterways of Europe and North America?

The first vessel equipped with a steam engine was the Marquis de Jouffroy's *Pyroscaphe*. For 15 minutes in 1783, she steamed up the River Saône near Lyon. Then she promptly broke down because the engine was far from perfect and extremely fragile.

In the late 1780s John Fitch planned to start the first regular passenger and goods service in the United States with his steam-driven oared boat. However, his plans came to nothing because the cargo space was small and the engine often broke down.

In 1802 William Symington built the *Charlotte Dundas* to tow barges on the Caledonian Canal and the River Clyde. However, the Canal Company banned his boat because they said her wake would damage the sides of the canal.

In 1812 Henry Bell's *Comet* began a regular passenger and goods service on the Clyde between Glasgow and Greenock. The fare in those days was three or four shillings (equivalent to 15 or 20p).

The first paddle-steamer to cross the Atlantic under steam only—from London to New York—was the 700-tonne *Sirius*. The crossing was made in 1838 at an average speed of 6.7 knots. In fair weather she could make 9 knots. These vessels were sailing ships fitted with steam engines. *Savannah* had crossed the Atlantic ahead of *Sirius*, but she had used her engines—for just 85 hours in a crossing lasting 29 days.

LINERS

By 1850 it was realized that not only were iron ships the safest and the most durable, but the most economical as well. In 1858 Isambard Kingdom Brunel demonstrated the potential of iron in shipbuilding with his *Great Eastern*, the most spectacular vessel ever to have been built up to that time. She was 211m long, 25m wide and displaced 27,400 tonnes fully loaded. Her two paddle-wheels and her screw (7m in diameter) could take her up to 13 knots. She had berths for 4,000 passengers and her bunkers carried 12,000 tonnes of coal, enough fuel to take her to India and back round the Cape of Good Hope. However, the

Great Eastern was technically so far ahead of her time that she proved an economic disaster. Banned from ports which she was too large to enter, she never operated in the role for which she was designed and, after laying the transatlantic telegraph cable, she ended her days as an exhibition ship.

Did you know...

... that the ocean liner *Queen Elizabeth II*, 65,800 tonnes, launched in 1968, now fills the more humble role of cruise liner, for which she was never designed?

Brunel's unfortunate experience with the *Great Eastern* gave naval architects second thoughts about the size of liners. In 1871 the launching of the *Oceanic*, 128m overall, set the pattern for this type of vessel. Her cabins were pleasingly arranged, comfortable, well lit and ventilated, thus making the whole voyage a pleasant experience.

The *Mauretania*, launched in 1906, was the first passenger vessel to be equipped with steam turbines. With her speed of just under 28 knots, she held the Blue Riband of the Atlantic, the symbolic award for the fastest crossing. Like her sister-ship the *Lusitania*, she measured 240m overall, 27m in breadth, and weighed 38,000 tonnes. Her turbines generated 70,000hp.

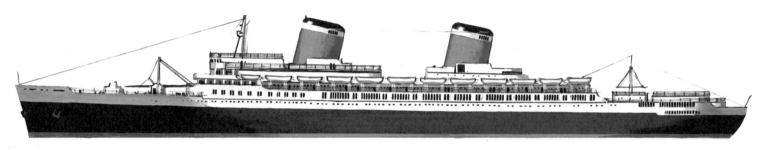

After World War II the Americans decided to snatch the Blue Riband and in 1950 built the *United States*. 300m long and with a gross tonnage of 53,000, in 1952 she set up a new transatlantic record of 3 days, 10 hours. Her 165,000hp engines enabled her to reach a speed of 37 knots. In 1969 she was laid up in honourable retirement.

The big liners admitted defeat when air transport made them uneconomic. In spite of this, the French as a matter of national prestige launched the 66,350-tonne *France* in 1960. She was withdrawn from service in 1975.

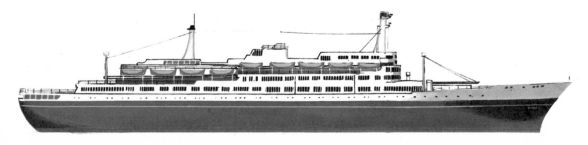

The future of liners lies in their being able to entertain passengers with time to spare in ever-increasing luxury. The *Rotterdam*, built in Holland in 1960 with a speed of under 20 knots, embodies all the qualities of a 'floating hotel'.

BATTLESHIPS

Because they carried the heaviest guns and the thickest armour, battleships were considered the rulers of the waves up to World War II. Their forerunners, the ironclads, were needed to give reasonable protection to wooden ships against the effects of the heavy rifled artillery pieces which were coming into service by the middle of the nineteenth century. The only answer to their vulnerability was to cover the most exposed portions of the hull with iron or steel plates. Thanks to advances in the steel industry, the earliest ironclads could be given armoured belts 100mm thick which transformed them into real floating fortresses. From the start, the development of the ironclad was closely linked with the development of the marine engine and the screw propeller, since naval authorities never favoured the paddle wheel. By the beginning of the twentieth century, the battleship was a formidable instrument of war.

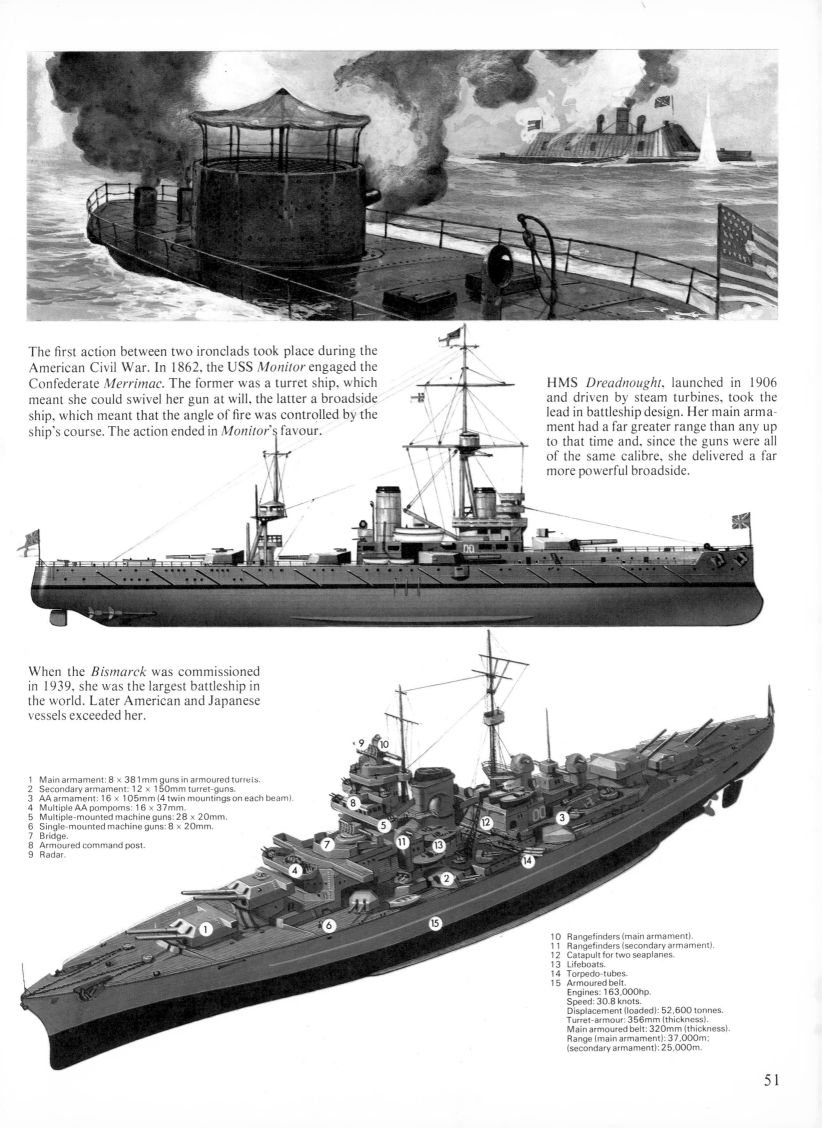

The first action between two ironclads took place during the American Civil War. In 1862, the USS *Monitor* engaged the Confederate *Merrimac*. The former was a turret ship, which meant she could swivel her gun at will, the latter a broadside ship, which meant that the angle of fire was controlled by the ship's course. The action ended in *Monitor*'s favour.

HMS *Dreadnought*, launched in 1906 and driven by steam turbines, took the lead in battleship design. Her main armament had a far greater range than any up to that time and, since the guns were all of the same calibre, she delivered a far more powerful broadside.

When the *Bismarck* was commissioned in 1939, she was the largest battleship in the world. Later American and Japanese vessels exceeded her.

1 Main armament: 8 × 381mm guns in armoured turrets.
2 Secondary armament: 12 × 150mm turret-guns.
3 AA armament: 16 × 105mm (4 twin mountings on each beam).
4 Multiple AA pompoms: 16 × 37mm.
5 Multiple-mounted machine guns: 28 × 20mm.
6 Single-mounted machine guns: 8 × 20mm.
7 Bridge.
8 Armoured command post.
9 Radar.

10 Rangefinders (main armament).
11 Rangefinders (secondary armament).
12 Catapult for two seaplanes.
13 Lifeboats.
14 Torpedo-tubes.
15 Armoured belt.
     Engines: 163,000hp.
     Speed: 30.8 knots.
     Displacement (loaded): 52,600 tonnes.
     Turret-armour: 356mm (thickness).
     Main armoured belt: 320mm (thickness).
     Range (main armament): 37,000m;
     (secondary armament): 25,000m.

THE INVISIBLE FOE

The idea of sailing under the water is very old, but the difficulties posed by it were not overcome until the end of the nineteenth century. Earlier experimental models had all been failures because of their lack of range. By World War I the submarine was a fully-fledged weapon and the German U-boats took a heavy toll of Allied shipping. They repeated their success in World War II when the Americans were equally successful against the Japanese. Below is an American submarine of the Cat class. It dates from 1941.

Did you know...

... that Jules Verne foresaw the submarine with the *Nautilus* in his book *20,000 Leagues Under the Sea*?

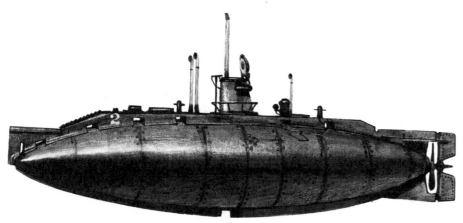

The Spaniard Isaac Peral's submarine. Launched in 1888 and powered only by electric motors, its range was restricted to about 200km. Within these limits it functioned efficiently and was equipped with accurate torpedoes. But the Spaniards did not appreciate its potentialities and it was never developed.

An early twentieth-century submarine. Its petrol engines for surface propulsion gave it a range of 2,800km. However, petrol fumes caused explosions and in 1909 diesel engines were substituted and became the standard power unit.

A World War II German U-boat. The cutaway section shows the crew's quarters, the inner hull (built to withstand pressures at depths of 200m) and the streamlined outer hull which held the ballast tanks.

By 1944 nearly all the German U-boats were fitted with schnorkel tubes through which they could 'breathe' and thus recharge their batteries without coming to the surface.

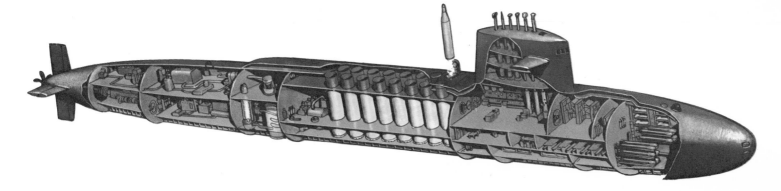

Today most submarines are nuclear-powered and this gives them an almost limitless range. They are able to sail several times round the world without coming to the surface. They are true submarines, unlike their predecessors which could travel under water for only part of their voyages and therefore were merely submersible vessels.

AIRCRAFT-CARRIERS

The aircraft-carrier is the warship which has driven the battleship off the seas. It can deliver bombs and torpedoes from well outside the long range even of the battleship's big guns. It proved its effectiveness in the major actions between the Japanese and the Americans in the Pacific in World War II when the two fleets were never in sight of one another. Below, HMS *Indomitable* in the Indian Ocean in 1942.

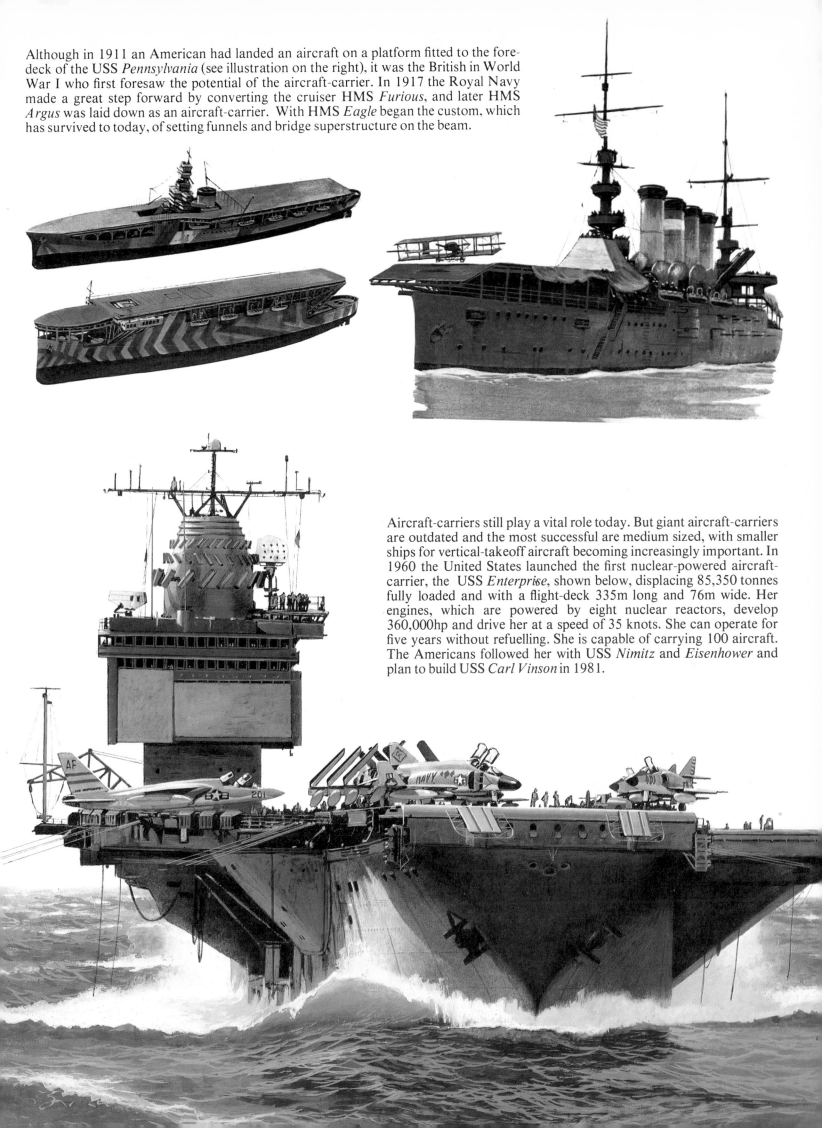

Although in 1911 an American had landed an aircraft on a platform fitted to the fore-deck of the USS *Pennsylvania* (see illustration on the right), it was the British in World War I who first foresaw the potential of the aircraft-carrier. In 1917 the Royal Navy made a great step forward by converting the cruiser HMS *Furious*, and later HMS *Argus* was laid down as an aircraft-carrier. With HMS *Eagle* began the custom, which has survived to today, of setting funnels and bridge superstructure on the beam.

Aircraft-carriers still play a vital role today. But giant aircraft-carriers are outdated and the most successful are medium sized, with smaller ships for vertical-takeoff aircraft becoming increasingly important. In 1960 the United States launched the first nuclear-powered aircraft-carrier, the USS *Enterprise*, shown below, displacing 85,350 tonnes fully loaded and with a flight-deck 335m long and 76m wide. Her engines, which are powered by eight nuclear reactors, develop 360,000hp and drive her at a speed of 35 knots. She can operate for five years without refuelling. She is capable of carrying 100 aircraft. The Americans followed her with USS *Nimitz* and *Eisenhower* and plan to build USS *Carl Vinson* in 1981.

MERCHANT SHIPS

Steam, building in iron and the screw propeller were the essentials of the new type of merchant ship. It was to be the pattern for the future and to all intents and purposes is still with us. In 1870 the typical merchant steamer had the same flush deck from stem to stern as the sailing ships of the period, but with bridge, funnel and engines amidships for the sake of stability. In those days seamen did not put their trust completely in mechanical power, so steamers still had sails.

Superstructures were introduced gradually: a wheelhouse was set on the stern and in the bows the peak was built up to house the anchors and act as a breakwater in bad weather. Then the bridge became larger and carried the helm. By 1880 merchant steamers had taken on the shape still seen today, as we can see from the illustration below showing an 1885 cargo ship of 1,500 tonnes.

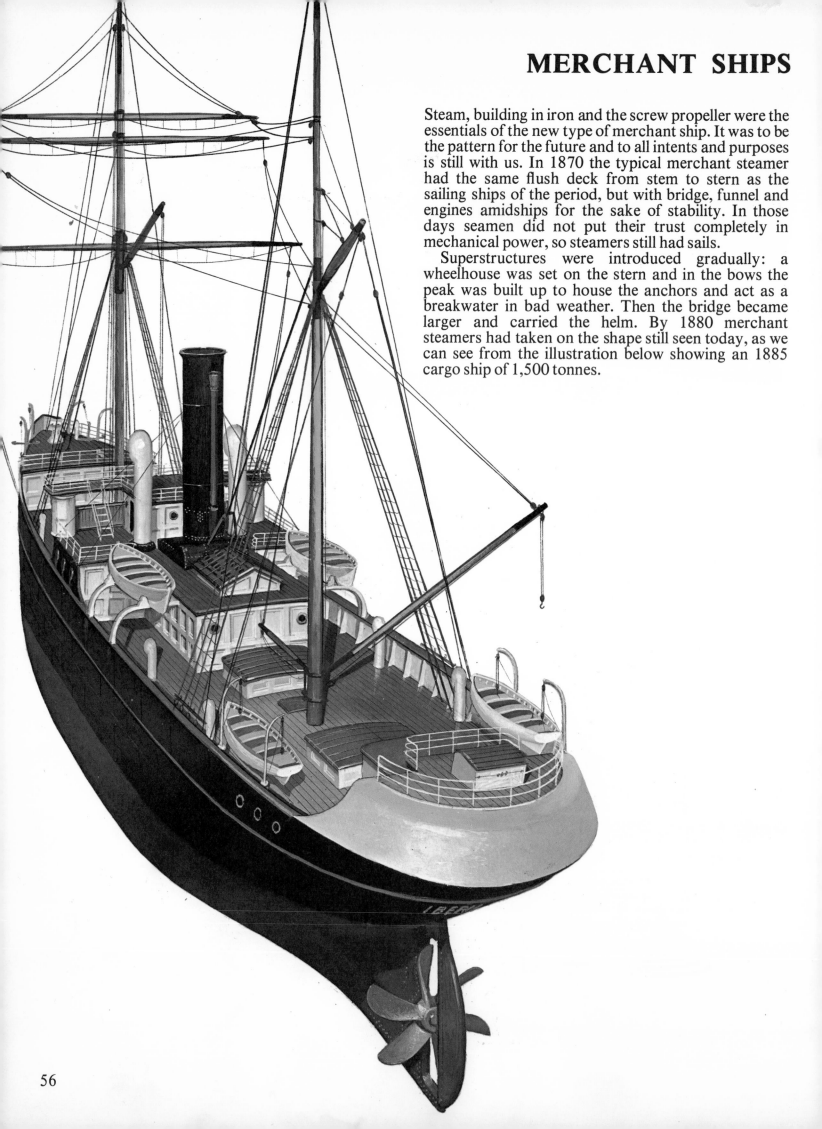

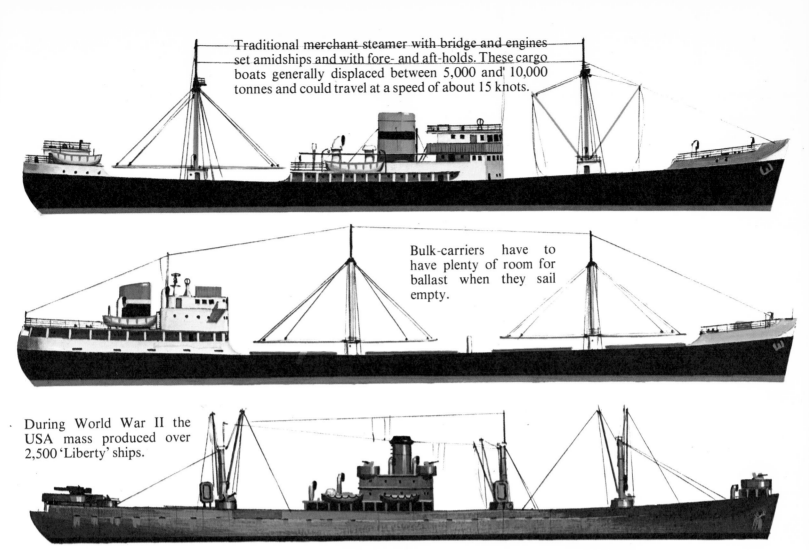

Traditional merchant steamer with bridge and engines set amidships and with fore- and aft-holds. These cargo boats generally displaced between 5,000 and 10,000 tonnes and could travel at a speed of about 15 knots.

Bulk-carriers have to have plenty of room for ballast when they sail empty.

During World War II the USA mass produced over 2,500 'Liberty' ships.

Today, tankers have become very important. The Japanese, who specialize in building super-tankers, have put the *Tokyo Maru*, with a displacement of 500,000 tonnes, into service. They planned to build a million-tonne tanker measuring 500m overall, but world economic conditions discourage the building of such giants and favour mixed carriers.

Merchant fleets are in process of developing along highly specialized lines with specific types of vessel for different cargoes—such as liquid gas, timber or bananas—as well as bulk-carriers, car-carriers and refrigerated ships, among many others. The illustration on the left shows the highly adaptable container-ship *Atlantic Cognac*, launched in 1970.

57

ICE-BREAKERS

For centuries man tried to sail the Arctic seas, but was always prevented by the layer of pack-ice covering them. Then he found that vessels with blunt bows were better able to break through the ice than those built on slender, raking lines. When the Royal Navy began to explore the Polar regions in the eighteenth century, they chose stoutly built bomb-ships for the task. Yet, however sturdy they were, sooner or later they became trapped in the ice.

The first vessel built to withstand pack-ice was the Norwegian explorer Nansen's *Fram*, while the first ice-breaker, in the modern sense of the term, was the Russian *Ermak*. The ice-breaker steams full-speed-ahead into the ice when her specially designed and reinforced prow rides up onto the pack and the weight of the vessel breaks it to clear a passage.

The hulls of ice-breakers are broad and specially strengthened, with a semicircular cross-section. They bulge at the bows so that the ship will not be trapped in the ice. The atomic ice-breaker *Lenin* can force a channel 30m wide through pack-ice 2-4m thick at a steady speed of 3 or 4 knots.

The Russian ice-breaker *Ermak*, launched in 1898.

FISHING BOATS

Fishing has always been a vital industry. The most modern ocean-going factory-ships, equipped with sonar and every other device, exist alongside humble inshore fishing vessels. One method of fishing is trawling. Ocean-going trawlers are fast sea-keeping vessels, for speed is, as ever, essential to reach the grounds quickly, shoot the nets and take full advantage of the shoals of fish. Vessels which make the long round trip out into the Atlantic or northern seas are built to stand up to storms and heavy seas.

TUGS

Tugs are small, powerful craft designed to tow or push other vessels. In antiquity, the Egyptians used tugs for towing purposes. The first modern tug was the *Charlotte Dundas*, which in the early 1800s pulled barges on the Forth and Clyde Canal in Scotland. A very useful and most practical craft, the tug has evolved in the same way as other vessels. Tugs retained paddle wheels until the early twentieth century. Because paddle wheels could be reversed, they were much more useful for manoeuvring in enclosed waters.

A modern tug.

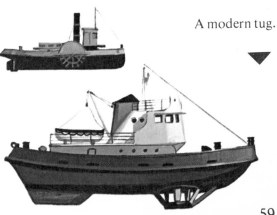

SPEED

The Hovercraft, also known as an air-cushion vehicle, moves on a cushion of air between it and the surface over which it travels. It was invented in the 1950s by Christopher Cockerell, who himself crossed the English Channel in 1959 in his first experimental model, the 3.8-tonne SRN-1. After various improvements had been made, the Hovercraft became a working proposition in the 1960s, but so far its use has been confined to ferry operations across relatively narrow stretches of water. A number of large-size Hovercraft have been brought into service, including the 167-tonne SRN-4. They maintain a most efficient, safe and speedy cross-Channel ferry service for passengers and vehicles.

The hydrofoil is a vessel with a hull which is built on traditional lines but equipped with winglike supports (its 'foils'), placed at right-angles to the centre-line. When the vessel gets up speed these foils force the live-works (all that part of the vessel normally below the waterline) to lift out of the water so that the craft glides over the surface on its foils. This reduces water resistance to a minimum and enables the hydrofoil to reach a speed of as much as 130km/h, or else to operate at the same speed as any normal fast ship but with half the power. Designers are planning to produce 500-tonne hydrofoils travelling at 200km/h.